T0321230

THE
LITTLE FROG'S
GUIDE TO
SELF-CARE

MAYBELL EEQUAY

summersdale

An Hachette UK Company
www.hachette.co.uk

Summersdale Publishers
Part of Octopus Publishing Group Limited
Carmelite House
50 Victoria Embankment
LONDON
EC4Y 0DZ
UK

www.summersdale.com

The authorized representative in the EEA is Hachette Ireland, 8 Castlecourt Centre, Dublin 15, D15 XTP3, Ireland (email: info@hbgi.ie)

Printed and bound in China

ISBN: 978-1-83799-101-3

This FSC® label means that materials used for the product have been responsibly sourced

MIX
Paper | Supporting responsible forestry
FSC® C016973

Substantial discounts on bulk quantities of Summersdale books are available to corporations, professional associations and other organizations. For details contact general enquiries: telephone: +44 (0) 1243 771107 or email: enquiries@summersdale.com.

FOR MOM AND JUJU,

THANK YOU FOR HOLDING ME DURING
THE HARD TIMES AND FOR ALWAYS
HELPING ME FIND MY WAY OUT. YOUR LOVE
AND YOUR LESSONS WILL BE WITH ME
AND INSPIRE ME FOREVER.

AND MY SWEET DRUE,

THIS LITTLE FROG WOULDN'T EXIST
WITHOUT YOU. I LOVE YOU.
I LOVE YOU. I LOVE YOU.

SELF-CARE FOR HARD TIMES

IF HOUSEHOLD OR SELF-CARE
TASKS FEEL TOO BIG, TRY
DOING THEM HALFWAY.

SOMETIMES WHEN WE'RE REALLY
STRUGGLING, SOMETHING AS
SIMPLE AS MAKING YOUR BED
CAN FEEL LIKE A CHALLENGE.

TO TAKE A LITTLE PRESSURE OFF
WHILE STILL GIVING YOURSELF EVEN A
SMALL FEELING OF ACCOMPLISHMENT,
TRY JUST STRAIGHTENING UP YOUR
BED INSTEAD OF FULLY MAKING IT.

IF YOUR HOUSE IS A MESS
AND IT FEELS OVERWHELMING,
START BY DOING JUST ONE
THING. THIS COULD BE TIDYING
UP ONE ROOM, OR IT COULD
BE SOMETHING EVEN SMALLER
LIKE CLEARING A TABLE. LITTLE
ACCOMPLISHMENTS ADD UP,
SO WHEN YOUR MENTAL
HEALTH ISN'T AT ITS BEST, TRY
FOCUSING ON ONE SMALL GOAL
AT A TIME TO HELP YOU GET
TO A BETTER HEADSPACE.

IF YOU HAVE DISHES PILING UP
AND DON'T HAVE THE ENERGY TO
CLEAN THEM, SOAK THEM IN SOAPY
WATER UNTIL YOU HAVE THE TIME
OR ENERGY. IT WILL MAKE CLEANING
THEM SO MUCH EASIER LATER.

IF YOU'RE FEELING LONELY, TRY WRITING
A LETTER TO SOMEONE WHO HAS HAD A
POSITIVE IMPACT ON YOUR LIFE. IT COULD
BE A RELATIVE, A FRIEND, A TEACHER, CO-
WORKER OR A LOVED ONE WHO HAS PASSED
AWAY (YOU DON'T HAVE TO SEND IT TO
THEM, BUT YOU CAN IF YOU WANT TO).

TAKING THE TIME TO SIT DOWN AND
APPRECIATE SOMEONE IN YOUR LIFE IS AN
EASY WAY TO BRING A LITTLE SWEETNESS
AND COMFORT INTO YOUR DAY.

IF YOU WANT YOUR DAY TO
FEEL A LITTLE MORE SPECIAL,
PICK SOME FLOWERS AND
DISPLAY THEM IN A VASE, OR
DRAW YOURSELF A WARM
BATH AND ADD SOME
PETALS TO THE WATER.

IF YOU WANT TO BUILD
A BETTER RELATIONSHIP
WITH YOUR BODY,
TRY THANKING IT.

THANK THE PARTS OF
YOUR BODY THAT YOU
USE A LOT OR THE
PARTS THAT YOU
JUDGE THE MOST.

MAYBE GIVE YOURSELF
A LITTLE HUG TOO.

IF YOU WANT TO BUILD
A BETTER RELATIONSHIP
WITH YOUR MIND, TRY
ADJUSTING YOUR SELF-TALK.

EVEN IF IT FEELS WEIRD OR
INAUTHENTIC AT FIRST,
OVER TIME YOU WILL
LIKELY START TO SEE A
DIFFERENCE IN THE WAY
YOU TREAT YOURSELF AND
IN THE WAY YOU ALLOW
OTHERS TO TREAT YOU.

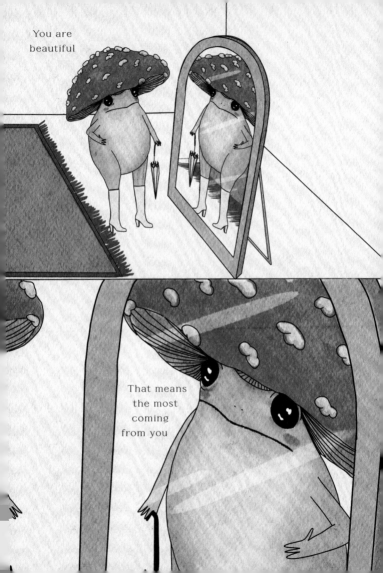

IF BEING KIND TO
YOURSELF FEELS
IMPOSSIBLE, TRY TO
FIND LOVE AND
COMPASSION FOR A
YOUNGER VERSION
OF YOURSELF.

SOMETIMES THINKING
ABOUT "LITTLE YOU"
WITH LOVE AND
COMPASSION CAN BE
EASIER THAN FEELING
THAT WAY TOWARDS
YOUR CURRENT SELF.

IF YOU WANT TO GO A LITTLE
DEEPER, TRY WRITING A LOVE
LETTER TO A VERSION OF
YOURSELF THAT WAS STRUGGLING.

IMAGINE IF THAT VERSION OF YOU
COULD READ THE LETTER. WHAT
WOULD YOU WANT TO TELL THEM?
THIS CAN BE A POWERFUL WAY
TO CONNECT WITH YOURSELF.

IF YOU HAVE A HARD TIME PRIORITIZING YOURSELF, TRY TO SET ASIDE AT LEAST FIVE MINUTES A DAY TO CREATE AN INTENTIONAL MOMENT OF "ME TIME".

YOU COULD EVEN REFRAME SOMETHING THAT IS ALREADY PART OF YOUR DAY LIKE DRINKING YOUR COFFEE OR TEA, DOING A SKIN-CARE ROUTINE, READING A COUPLE OF PAGES OF A BOOK OR SITTING OUTSIDE.

BONUS POINTS IF IT'S WITHOUT YOUR PHONE.

TEN AFFIRMATIONS TO REMIND YOU OF THE MAGIC THAT YOU HOLD

IF YOU ARE BUILDING A HEALTHY RELATIONSHIP WITH YOURSELF AND WORKING ON ADJUSTING YOUR SELF-TALK, AFFIRMATIONS ARE A GREAT PLACE TO START.

I'M GOING
TO BE
NICER TO
MYSELF.

I AM AS
WORTHY OF
MY DREAMS
AS ANYONE
ELSE.

MY BODY
WORKS
SO HARD
FOR ME.

MAGIC ALWAYS
REVEALS ITSELF
WHEN I'M WILLING
TO SEE IT.

I AM WORTHY OF
SAFE AND HEALTHY
RELATIONSHIPS.

I AM ALLOWED TO
FEEL THE EMOTIONS
THAT ARE MOVING
THROUGH ME, AND I
AM ALLOWED TO LET
GO OF THEM WHEN
I AM READY.

I WILL BE
GENTLE WITH
MYSELF.

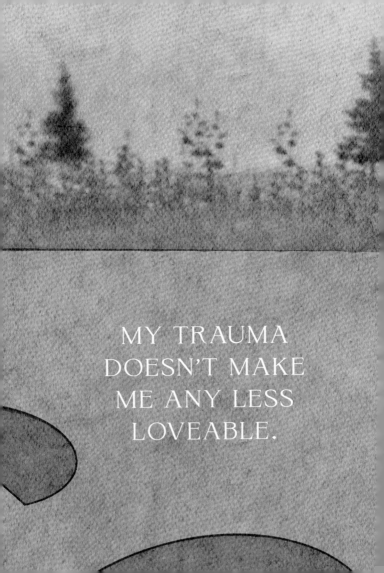

MY TRAUMA
DOESN'T MAKE
ME ANY LESS
LOVEABLE.

I AM GOING TO
TREAT MYSELF THE
WAY I WOULD TREAT
MY BEST FRIEND.

ALLOWING AND
ENCOURAGING
YOURSELF TO
FIND MAGIC IN
THE WORLD
AROUND YOU

WITH EVERYTHING
GOING ON IN THE WORLD
IT CAN BE EASY TO FORGET
ABOUT ALL THE LITTLE
THINGS THAT MAKE LIFE
ON EARTH SO SPECIAL.

TINY MIRACLES ARE
HAPPENING IN EVERY
MOMENT, AND TAPPING INTO
THEM CAN CHANGE THE
WAY THAT YOU SEE THE
WORLD AROUND YOU.

HAVE YOU EVER SAT AND QUIETLY
OBSERVED A GARDEN BEFORE?

THE LONGER YOU LOOK, THE MORE LIFE
YOU START TO SEE. TINY, INTRICATE
WORLDS BEGIN TO REVEAL THEMSELVES,
AND SUDDENLY GARDENS FEEL SO MUCH
MORE ALIVE THAN THEY DID BEFORE.

SIMPLE THINGS START TO FEEL EXTRAORDINARY WHEN YOU LOOK AT THEM WITH CURIOSITY AND WONDER.

I can't believe
pine cones exist

CAN YOU BELIEVE
THAT WE GET TO
LIVE ON THE SAME
PLANET AS FIREFLIES?
THAT ALONE FEELS
LIKE A REASON FOR
CELEBRATION.

OR HAVE YOU EVER CONSIDERED HOW SURREAL IT IS THAT WE ARE ABLE TO HAVE ANIMALS AS COMPANIONS? EVEN THOUGH WE DON'T SPEAK THE SAME LANGUAGE AS THEM WE ARE ABLE TO FIND WAYS TO COMMUNICATE WITH EACH OTHER, AND SOMETIMES THOSE BONDS ARE EVEN DEEPER THAN THOSE WITH OTHER HUMANS.

AS WE GROW UP AND OUR UNDERSTANDING OF THE WORLD STARTS TO FORM, IT'S EASY TO STOP WONDERING. WHY ARE SOME LEAVES GREEN, WHILE OTHERS ARE PURPLE OR RED? ARE SNAILS BORN WITH SHELLS? WHY DO SOME FLOWERS BLOOM AT NIGHT? OF COURSE, WITH THE INTERNET WE CAN FIND ANSWERS TO ALL THESE QUESTIONS WITHIN SECONDS, BUT LETTING YOURSELF THINK ABOUT IT FIRST CAN HELP YOU STAY CURIOUS, AND IT MIGHT EVEN SPARK A GENUINE INTEREST IN SOMETHING YOU'VE NEVER REALLY THOUGHT ABOUT BEFORE.

TRY TO FIND SOMETHING THAT YOU LOVE
AND LOOK FORWARD TO IN EACH SEASON.

THE WAY THAT THE AIR SMELLS IN AUTUMN
OR HOW THE WINTER MONTHS GIVE US
THE OPPORTUNITY TO COZY UP AND GO
INWARD. THE WAY THAT EVERY SPRING
IT FEELS LIKE THE WORLD IS WAKING UP
FROM A DEEP SLEEP OR HOW SUMMER IS
ALWAYS SO VIBRANT AND FULL OF LIFE.

FINDING WAYS TO EMBRACE EACH OF
THE SEASONS GIVES YOU SOMETHING
TO FEEL GOOD ABOUT ANY TIME
OF YEAR, EVEN IF IT'S SMALL.

TRY GOING OUTSIDE
WITH THE INTENTION
TO JUST BE PRESENT.
WHAT DO YOU HEAR?
WHAT DO YOU SEE?
WHAT DOES THE AIR
SMELL LIKE? WHAT
DO YOU FEEL?

HOW DO YOU FEEL?

ALLOWING YOURSELF
TO FIND MAGIC IN THE
LITTLE THINGS IS ONE
OF THE SWEETEST WAYS
YOU CAN INTERACT
WITH THE WORLD.
WHEN YOU LOOK FOR
IT, YOU'LL FIND IT.

THINGS TO
REMEMBER

ALL EMOTIONS SERVE A PURPOSE:
SADNESS, ANGER, GRIEF, JOY,
AWE, SERENITY AND SO ON.

ALTHOUGH SOME EMOTIONS ARE LESS FUN
TO FEEL THAN OTHERS, THAT DOESN'T
MEAN THAT THEY ARE BAD. PART OF BEING
HUMAN IS FEELING A WIDE SPECTRUM
OF EMOTIONS THROUGHOUT YOUR LIFE.
THEY'LL ALL COME AND GO, AND EVEN IF
IT'S HARD TO BELIEVE IN THE MOMENT,
THE HARD ONES WON'T LAST FOREVER.

YOUR PROGRESS IS
NOT DIMINISHED BY
YOUR SETBACKS.

DESPITE HOW IT MAY
SEEM, THERE IS NO
PERFECT FORMULA FOR
LIFE, AND EVERYONE
AROUND YOU IS,
FOR THE MOST PART,
FIGURING IT OUT
AS THEY GO.

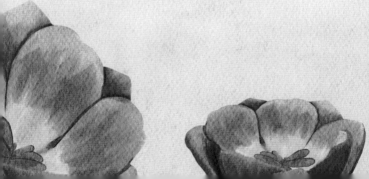

WE'RE ALL ON OUR OWN TIMELINES AND THERE ARE NO ACTUAL RULES THAT DETERMINE WHERE YOU SHOULD BE IN LIFE BY A CERTAIN AGE.

YOUR THOUGHTS
AREN'T ALWAYS TRUE.
ANXIETY, DEPRESSION,
INSECURITIES AND
MORE CAN INFLUENCE
OUR THOUGHTS IN
MANY WAYS AND IT'S
IMPORTANT TO REMEMBER
THAT JUST BECAUSE
WE THINK IT, IT DOESN'T
MEAN THAT IT IS A FACT.

THE PROCESS OF
HEALING IS RARELY
LINEAR AND IT'S
OKAY TO CRY ABOUT
SOMETHING THAT YOU
THOUGHT YOU HAD
HEALED FROM.

YOU DON'T NEED
TO RETURN TO
PAST VERSIONS OF
YOURSELF TO SATISFY
PEOPLE WHO AREN'T
READY TO SEE HOW
YOU'VE GROWN.

CHOSEN FAMILY
IS REAL FAMILY.

YOU NEED TO BE THE
ONE TO GIVE YOURSELF
PERMISSION TO BECOME
THE PERSON THAT
YOU WANT TO BE.

THERE ARE SO MANY
BIG AND HARD THINGS
HAPPENING IN THE
WORLD, AND THERE
MAY BE PERSONAL
HARDSHIPS WE
MUST ENDURE, BUT
IT'S IMPORTANT TO
REMEMBER THAT YOU
ARE NOT ALONE AND
THAT IT'S OKAY TO
NOT BE OKAY.

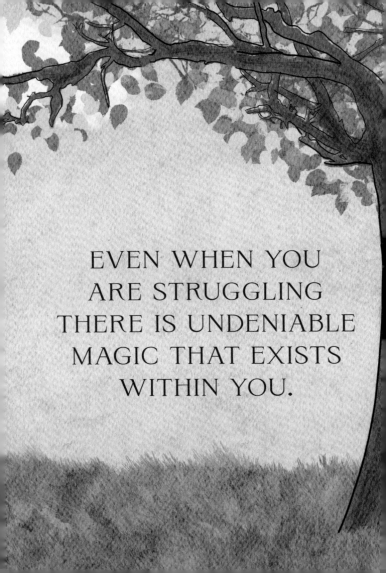

EVEN WHEN YOU
ARE STRUGGLING
THERE IS UNDENIABLE
MAGIC THAT EXISTS
WITHIN YOU.

AT THE END OF THE DAY, WE ARE ALL JUST A BUNCH OF TINY FROGS FLOATING THROUGH SPACE TOGETHER, TRYING TO MAKE EACH OTHER FEEL A LITTLE LESS ALONE AND OUR TIME HERE A LITTLE MORE SPECIAL.

ABOUT THE
AUTHOR

Maybell Eequay is an Oakland-based artist who works in many different mediums. Born and raised in the breathtaking St Croix River Valley, Maybell draws a lot of inspiration from her childhood home life as well as her love of vintage children's books and knickknacks. Growing up in a creative household and the daughter of two artists, Maybell has been making art since she was old enough to hold a pen. Today, she enjoys making art that has a vaguely nostalgic feel paired with tender messages and light humour.

Find Maybell on Instagram at
@maybell.eequay

Have you enjoyed this book?

If so, find us on Facebook at
Summersdale Publishers, on Twitter at
@Summersdale and on Instagram and TikTok at
@summersdalebooks and get in touch.

We'd love to hear from you!

www.summersdale.com